THIS BOOK DONATED BY:

The 6th Grade
Class
of
1993

What Once Was White

Written by Samantha Abeel

Watercolors by Charles R. Murphy

Edited by Roberta Williams

Hidden Bay Publishing

Traverse City, Michigan

Publisher's Cataloging in Publication Data

Abeel, Samantha.
  What Once Was White/by Samantha Abeel; illustrated by Charles R. Murphy; edited
by Roberta Williams.
    1, Literature . 2, Inspiration. 3, Education
    I. Murphy, Charles R., ill.   II. Title
    Summary: A collection of art and poetry written by a young girl; essays by her teacher
and parent map the journey of her struggle with a learning disability.

Published by Hidden Bay Publishing, P.O. Box 86 , Traverse City, MI 49685-0086

Printed in the United States of America
FIRST EDITION

Library of Congress Catalog Card Number: 93-77359

ISBN 0-941653-13-7

Dedicated to those who daily struggle with "differences", no matter what they are, and to those who labor to help them.

Wellspring

If you want to fill the well, make a boat out of paper,
set it on a dry, and dusty river bed,
cracked and wrinkled like the face of a grandmother.
Lie down on its fragile planks,
spread your hair over the edge like ivy
to cling to the broken sand

Let your thoughts begin to trickle
as if they were rain,
soaking your clothes and hair
until you feel yourself begin to drift along
on the current of ideas
like a leaf fallen on a river

Spinning across reflections of the sky
and eddying through the willows,
find the current below you,
seeking its way into the ancient stone edifice of the well,
pouring into its empty circle
just as love pours into an empty heart

The well becomes full
and your words are lifted in a bucket -
brought into the sunlight
where the thirsty dip their hands in and drink.

Welcome to an unusual book. If you have ever struggled to overcome the impossible, to be heard in spite of those who would silence you, or to be understood by those who held your fate in their hands, you will find encouragement here. When the idea for this book was conceived, Samantha was twelve years old and striving to cope with a learning disability that threatened to smother her. She could not tell time, count money, remember simple mathematical concepts or spell. Yet she had a voice inside her that would not be silenced.

Her voice was encouraged to grow with a simple idea, a summer writing activity inspired by the watercolors of Charles R. Murphy. It was conceived to focus on what was right with Samantha, in contrast to the many years of frustration in contending with what was wrong. The artist, a talented and notable painter, generously supplied Samantha with images that inspired her. Each of his paintings became an opportunity for her to use her gifted powers of observation and imagination. In the process, it became a book that has changed us all. As the paintings and poems took shape, we realized this book was not only about writing and painting, it was about education. It has become a reminder that the learning disabled are not ignorant, lazy or hopeless; they can be sensitive, intelligent people who learn differently. They, like Samantha, must have tremendous perseverance to master what seem like basic skills to others.

For those who look at words and see only an impossible confusion of lines, for those who live in fear of being asked to make change for a dollar, for those who look at the face of a clock and see only a blur of numbers and hands without meaning, this book offers inspiration. It speaks to what many parents and thoughtful educators have come to realize: it is not enough to address a child's strengths or weaknesses separately. An approach that allows focus on strengths, while addressing weaknesses, will help children to fulfill their *whole* potential.

As long as there are children who learn differently, a book like this can be an affirmation of the importance of their struggle. You will find here a striking collection of paintings that are classic Charles Murphy: imaginative, dashed with whimsy, and often surrounded by the arms of nurturing, embracing figures whose presence is found in the most common of objects and forces around us. They provided the visual nudge for Samantha. In his words, "A painting heavily loaded or ripe in symbolism carries a hundred sentences on its back and speaks paragraphs to its viewers." What he paints, she translates into words. Together, they help us view the special inner world they see surrounding us all.

What Once Was White

Emptiness no longer prevails, her song has now begun

The harmony calls forth images

and as she weaves her melodic tune,

his brush keeps frantic time

Sweeping the canvas, each note becomes a swirling color

What once was white is transformed

and a new world flows forth

Silver notes become strands of her hair,

entwining fish which wave and weave among the brush strokes

Butterfly wings emerge from the treble clef

painting jewels upon her robe which shimmer like wet paint

A noble oak springs from the bass clef

reaching in supplication for the tip of the brush

The canvas becomes a place where songs are pictures

and pictures are symphonies

Harmony and color combine,

creating windows to a life within a life

Immortality swells with each note

Sunrise

Silently in the darkness
pale and hushed
I dream about this still cold world.
Opening my eyes,
waiting to part the curtain of night,
I ascend
and the grass, once black, is green-
stretching toward the sky.
The wind yawns through the trees
and I gently caress the darkness from their leaves
and whisper "Wake."
The birds take flight
carrying my light upon their wings.
I behold this newly born world
and whisper in the ears of those who
covet darkness,
"You can't keep out the light."

Alone

There is a place where we all go
when we must sit alone
A place where the birds are free to fly
A place where the sun and its flowers bow in shadow
A place where the fog is like a veil
and everything is protected
A place where our souls are set free
and we are allowed to play our own song

Quilt

In the sun, my grandmother would sit,
calico and gingham spread long,
like a river speckled in fall leaves,
over her skirt.
Slowly gathering the pieces,
bringing them all together
she would rock, needle in hand.
"Life is a quilt made of many different
faces,"
she used to say,
"a fabric
of different goals and dreams,
each with different colors,
different eyes,
different hands,
yet bound together by a single piece of thread."

Come All the Old

While the ocean above me uncovered its pearl and the village ceased its bustle and quieted under that spell called sleep, I looked out from my window to the street below. All was still and unmoving except for the moonlight that tripped over the cobbled stones as if it were a child at play. Like a figure in a dream, a man came walking down the street and as he stepped into the moonlight, I could see his face. His eyes were shaped like the sun as it sets below the sea. His face was rough and unshaven, like a field just after harvest. He looked old, but I couldn't tell how old. Upon his back he carried a cage full of chickens and birds, and on his head was an old lamp shade with several feathers jutting like blades of tall grass.

Stopping at the corner, he slowly removed the cage from his back and opened its little door. Bowing as if before a king, the old man watched each bird flutter onto the pavement. Silently he took from his sack a worn set of bagpipes.

Gingerly placing the mouthpiece to his thin lips, he began to play. At first, the notes seemed to wheeze, but soon they cleared and the bagpipe music danced before him down the street. Limply, an old bag woman hobbled by, causing the birds to flutter as she passed.

Suddenly, as if her head had been attached to a string, she raised it and after staring at the strange old man for a minute, she began to dance, sending the birds scattering. When the old man saw this, he began to play more rapidly and his music seemed to say, "Come all who have suffered, who have seen history's face, those who have been forgotten or for whom death is on its way. If life has done you good, then dance for joy. Come all the old and be young again." One by one the old people of the village arrived, lured by the sound of the music. Men who hadn't walked in years threw down their crutches, and women whose backs were bent by time were straightened. People who had been lying on their death beds were suddenly alive and full of energy. They danced among the birds, sending feathers flying. The old man led them down the cobbled street and into the darkness beyond, yet his music seemed to linger in the moonlight and whisper, "Come all the old and be young again."

Leaves in the Fall

They are the leaves in the fall,
the snow on the ground.
They are the wind in the trees,
the waves upon the sea.
They were our hopes and our dreams,
yet now their chairs are left empty,
their books unopened.

At first we did not notice the empty chairs,
or the unread stories.
We wanted to forget them,
like a child wants to forget his nightmares.
Now we realize our mistakes,
for they were heroes,
and we should honor them for what they gave,
and what they gave up.
A human life is a gift
more precious than anything,
and it should never be wasted.

We cannot just forget that they are no longer here,
that their voices will no longer be heard,
their smiles no longer seen.
We cannot just forget that they will never feel the sun
or count the stars,
for they were a part of us,
a part of our country.
They are the leaves in the fall,
the snow on the ground.
They are the dead of Viet Nam.

COURTADE LMC
TRAVERSE CITY, MI

Music of the Heart

Like shadows dancing in the light of a flickering candle, the waves rose from the mist, each one a ghost, gray and cold, trying desperately to touch the warmth of life. Yet just as its icy fingertips were about to claim victory, they were pulled back into the mist, back into the cold and gray, where they were forced to wait in the shadows until they were allowed to rise again.

Silently, my eyes scanned the curtain of mist looming about me; above, the fall sky was a dull gray. I sat down upon a tall and weathered rock and I could see by its deep cracks, that the lake had already scrolled out its name upon its rounded surface. Slowly, I bent down and picked up a feather that was lying next to me. I lifted it above my head and released it into the air. Silently, I watched as it spun upon the breeze and gently landed in the sand. It was then that I heard it, like a gentle whisper of a lullaby. It filled my ears. It was a violin song that seemed to be played by the wind. At first it sounded distant, but before I knew it, it was upon me, and I could feel its every note run like a river through my mind. I felt a gust upon my face. I turned, and there, sitting before me, was an old man, his face gathered in wrinkles and his hair hanging about him like cobwebs.

Slowly, he raised his black eyes to me. They were deep, almost never-ending, and within them I knew there was a message hiding in the darkness, but it seemed as if something prevented me from discovering it. In his hand he held a violin. "I knew you would come," he said in a voice like a spring breeze.

"Who are you?" I asked. "What do you mean, you knew I would..."

"Hush, hush, child," he said interrupting me. "I cannot hear the music when you talk!"

"What music?" I asked. "What are you talking about?"

"Why, the music being played by the waves. Now hush so I can listen."

We sat for a moment in total silence, then he picked up his violin and began to play. It was a song like no other, each note seeming to cry and to laugh, and with each emotion I was taken with it. After he finished, he began to smile. "Why do you not smile?" he asked. "Do you not hear? It is a joyful song!"

"What song?" I asked in confusion. "All I heard was your violin."

"My dear," he said, "forgive me. I did not know you were deaf, but I shall soon fix that." Vigorously he set his violin to his shoulder and began to play.

Like the spires of a steeple, the masts of long dead ships began to rise from their sandy graves below the lake and shoot up from the mist. Most of them were nothing but scattered pieces of wood, a few sails covering them like torrents of wet leaves. I felt myself begin to shake; everything was spinning, then all went black.

I must have fainted, for when I awoke, I was lying on the deck of a ship whose wood was well worn and whose mast was crying out like a raven. Slowly, I got up and went to the ship's railing. We were moving quickly, cutting through the waves like a knife. No land was in sight. It was then that I noticed a gaping hole in the ship's hull, and that there was but one sail ripped through the middle. Just then I heard a voice that seemed to creep up behind me, and with it a low, nearly inaudible violin song, "So you have awakened." It was the voice of the old man.

"Why have you brought me here?" I asked, growing angry. "What do you want from me?"

His black eyes looked into mine, searching. "My child, when I play the violin, I play it for the waves on the lake, for the gulls crying up above, and for those who have learned to listen with their heart and not their ears. For the ears only pick up the sounds from the surface, and not what is waiting beyond. You see, everything in life has a harmony, an ever-flowing song. For the moment, it is my music that keeps us afloat upon the coldness swirling below. Yet, my music cannot go on forever." He stopped playing. The whole ship lurched forward and I could hear the bottom begin to fill with water. "That is why you must learn to hear the eternal music of the heart and let it keep you afloat."

Just then the rain began to fall upon us and the waves grew high, moaning, reaching, grabbing at my ankles, trying to pull me down to their home below. "Keep playing!" I exclaimed. "We shall sink if you don't!" The old man just stood there, now barely visible through the driving rain and wind. "Are you crazy?" I yelled. "Keep playing!" I could feel the water. It was now to my waist and nothing but the mast of the ship rose above the waves. I moved toward it and grabbing hold, I felt myself sink with it.

The water rose to my ears, flooding them. My hand reached up to the sky, hoping to grab hold of the invisible when I heard it. The music of my heart. It rushed through me like the tide. Suddenly, the sky cleared, and I could feel the warmth of the sun upon me. The water became a glorious blue as the gray dissipated. I felt

myself being lifted and carried upon the waves, their wrath now settled. Gently, I was set upon the rock. Next to me lay the feather. The mist had disappeared and I could hear the music, not with my ears, but with my heart.

Voices of Ancestry

Voices in the canyon wind have uncovered my
deaf ears -
kind
pleading
strong
searching
wistful
caring
frightened
voices -
whispers of what used to be
before my ancestors left this canyon,
before they bled into the sea
and were lost.

Shivers in the Blackness

The lake is still and the trees stand silent for each has become a shadow . An eagle takes flight, his wings riding upon the promises of the past. From this darkness, his cry is picked up by the wind and taken to an ancient land. There, in the night, a hand is stretched out beckoning the eagle who appears from the darkness. It is the hand of a woman who comes with the night to hear the words that are spoken by the wind. In the dawn she will give them to her people. The eagle cries and the whispers begin. They are sighs as they pass her cheek turning into words and filling her ear. After they are spoken, they drift off among the strands of her hair and die. The words of the wind that are spoken this night are few, but full of truth. "Listen to the wisdom echoing from deep within your memories. Though it is hidden, it is always there. Feel for it through the darkness." The whispers then fade and the eagle spreads his wings to the dawn. As he disappears into the darkness of the future, a feather floats from the sky to land gently upon the surface of the lake, sending shivers through the blackness.

If You Want to See

If you want to see the past
look around you
for everything you do is
living out the legacy of those
who came before you...

        Feathers, the open plain
        a life following
        the heartbeat of a drum.
        Peace. Simplicity.
        The eyes of a people
        looking with hope,
        to the future.

If you want to see the present,
look around you
for it is what you are building
for those who will come
after you...

        Poverty, not enough room,
        the dreams have ended.
        Feathers float to the ground, and
        drums no longer beat their rhythm
        The eyes of a people
        look on with misgiving
        to the future.

If you want to see the future,
look inside you
for it is where all the building
begins.

The Cloak

I am old, the sun has set,
it is time for me to fade into the background of life
Death has given me his cloak to wear
Do not worry, for his cloak is warm and the chill north
wind can no longer harm me.
I can feel my soul as it is pulled from me and
taken to a place where it can be at
peace forever.
It is time. My breath becomes the falling
breeze, and my body the solid
stem; my arms become the branches
reaching to a higher grace, and my
hair unfolds into leaves of light.
I have entered the forest of
eternity and stand as a tree should.
A sigh passes from my lips
and all is still.
I am old,
and the sun
has set.

Drawing the Curtain of Night

Crumple the day, shred the sunlight and
scatter it into the sky
Summon clouds, shape into an alabaster mountain, then
sculpt his benign and powerful features.

Watch as with one hand he grasps the curtain of night,
drawing darkness over the edge of the earth.
In the hush, the world becomes still
waiting expectantly for the moon to kindle the sky.

Carefully, he suspends it amongst the stars
then stands back, appraising his work
before disappearing behind the curtain to
wait for the whisper of sunlight.

Samantha's Story...

Self Portrait by Samantha

Perspectives by her teacher and her mother

Self Portrait

To show you who I am
I crawled inside a tree, became its roots, bark and leaves,
listened to its whispers in the wind
When fall came and painted the leaves red and gold
I wanted to shake them across your lawn
to transform the grass into a quilt, a gift spread at your feet,
but their numbers eluded me,
so I turned a piece of paper into my soul
to send to you so that you might see
how easily it can be crumpled and flattened out again.
I wanted you to see my resilience,
but I wasn't sure how to arrange the numbers in your address,
so I danced with the Indians in the forest
and collected the feathers that fell from the eagle's wings,
each one a wish for my future,
but I lost track of their numbers, gathered too many,
and was unable to carry them home
so I reaped the wind with my hair,
relived its journey through my senses, and
felt its whispered loneliness, like lakes in winter,
but it was too far and you could not follow me.

Now I've written out their shadows
like the wind collects its secrets
to whisper into receptive ears, and I
will leave them at your doorstep,
a reminder of what others cannot see,
a reminder of what I can and cannot be.

From her teacher's view: addressing her strength

Have you ever received an unexpected gift? The kind that not only surprises but changes you? I have, though at the time I didn't recognize it as such. This gift was a child who combined unusual creative abilities with profound learning disabilities. The fact that one person could contain such opposites was a revelation and a challenge. In the process of meeting this challenge, I learned the importance of cultivating the gift so the disability could be faced with confidence. Because we were successful, I am pleased to be a part of introducing Samantha and her story to you. Her achievement and perseverance in spite of the obstacles she has had to overcome are remarkable.

When Samantha entered my seventh grade classroom in 1990, I saw a quiet, shy girl. Classes were large and I worried she would get lost. It didn't take long, however, for her to introduce herself in a compelling way. She wrote. The first writing seventh graders do is rarely memorable. Samantha's was an exception. The thought and insight she brought to the assignment showed she had a gift for writing I wanted to encourage. However, in spite of her agility with words and her capacity for insight, she struggled with spelling, verb tenses, word omissions and other mechanical problems. As I got to know her better, I learned these problems were insignificant compared to what she experienced in math. Watching her in my classroom where she excelled was to see a different child than the one who was completely intimidated in her math class. This paradox is what made Samantha difficult to categorize and therefore difficult to label.

Now that I am aware this dichotomy can exist, I have a suspicion there are more Samanthas in our classrooms: the quiet ones who hide out in the back, the ones who always "forget" their homework or are constantly apologizing, the ones who "cover" by distracting us with their behavior, their language, or their attitude. How much have we missed because we didn't have the right key, didn't know a key existed, didn't even know the door was locked?

"...a child who combined unusual creative abilities with profound learning disabilities...a paradox..."

"Slowly her confidence grew..."

For Samantha, that locked door caused tremendous problems. As Sally L. Smith says in her enlightening book, <u>Succeeding Against the Odds</u>, "A person with learning disabilities often carries a heavy burden of loneliness, feeling he is the only one in the whole world who has struggled so hard only to experience the pain of failure." It was important to me that Samantha didn't fail. While I was not qualified to help her with math, I could encourage her writing. We started to focus on what was right about her.

For English she used a word processor with a spell checker and I ignored left-out words and was patient with her mechanical difficulties - small prices to pay for the writing this twelve year old could produce. I also had to be flexible about due dates when she became overwhelmed. Because of her disability, overloads of work caused *every* area to short circuit. Rules are important, but it is equally important to know when to modify them.

Slowly, her confidence grew and she bloomed. At the end of her seventh grade year we didn't want to lose the momentum we had. I was getting the message from her mother that writing was Samantha's lifeline. That is when the idea of a summer spent writing was born. Her mother called me one day with a proposal. Would I be willing to give her writing lessons? Her logic was that if Samantha were interested in piano, she would encourage piano lessons. The confidence she had built through her writing during her seventh grade year needed to be sustained. We also felt it would be important to provide structured assignments to focus Samantha's time. In her case, more structure was actually release. What better way to do this than to reflect and write about the work of an artist we all admired. Charles Murphy was eager to encourage Samantha because he felt an empathy with her. He knew what it was like to be different, what it was like to be constantly discouraged. As a high school student, he had been denied art classes because he was on the college preparatory track. He had also been discouraged from pursuing an art career because the chances for successfully earning a living were so minimal. Thankfully he followed what he knew was right for him: he pursued what he did well. Art was the key that unlocked the door.

We wanted to accomplish the same with Samantha through her writing. When we started this project she had never written poetry before, yet her imagery rich language was perfect for expression in this medium. We went through boxes of slides of Charles' work and visited gallery openings and shows where we could see the paintings first hand. Insights and images poured from her. She was finally free to express what had been locked inside.

I'll never forget the first time we shared her writing with Charles. We were so nervous, wondering if she'd got it "right," if what she saw was justified by *his* perceptions of his work. Writing about paintings is not a new technique, but how many students are ever faced with sharing their interpretations face to face with the artist? Both of these remarkable people deserve special praise: Samantha for being courageous enough to share her inner world and Charles for accepting her offerings seriously, critically and as artist to artist. The poems were a success. At the same time, everywhere we turned were people who had learning experiences similar to Samantha's, many without the happy ending. We found that the paintings and poetry were striking a chord, but so was the chronicle of why they existed. We knew we needed to share the story of the journey there.

The more we worked, the more energized all of us became and now, the Samantha who sits in my ninth grade classroom is a much stronger, confident person than the girl I saw that first day two years ago. Because she has been given appropriate remediation in her problem areas and encouraged in her strengths, she has the self-confidence to confront her weaknesses. I hope Samantha's story can provide inspiration for those who are struggling to contend with their disabilities, and that it can also serve as a reminder to educators everywhere. When we look for possibilities and potential in every student, then nurture those qualities, all children can become successful learners. And that should be what we're all about.

Roberta Williams

"... everywhere we turned were people who had learning experiences similar to Samantha's, many without the happy ending."

From her mother's view: addressing the weakness

It started with a dead fish. While walking the beach one fall day, I turned to see my twenty-two month old daughter, Samantha, carefully studying the rotting remains of a salmon. When I went back to urge her on, she looked up at me and asked, "Is this what is going to happen to us?" Later, when she was four, she surprised us on a car trip by spontaneously reciting an hour long cassette story tape of *Star Wars*. Her delivery was flawless, including all multi-syllable words and tonal inflections. Her capacity to do this came as a total surprise.

Because of traits like these, we felt confident she would be a successful student in school. However, when kindergarten came we saw a very quiet and observant Samantha. As early as first grade, the child we knew as bright and imaginative was coming home scared and unhappy. How could this be?

Second grade brought concerns from her teacher. She seemed to need a little extra help in basic math. I will never forget that night in February. A simple flash card: 5-3=2 changed our lives. My bright, verbally agile daughter quite simply had no idea of 5, of 3, of 2. As a result of my frustration to "make her see," we were both in tears.

Thus began the educational roller coaster. I knew something was not right with Samantha's learning. She combined strength in her language and thought patterns with total confusion in numbers. Eager to know what could be done, I asked the school for help. I learned about the Individualized Educational Planning Committee or IEPC. This is a process by which children with suspected learning disabilities are evaluated to determine eligibility for special help. I wish I had known more about the significance of the IEPC procedure when Samantha was first tested. I knew so little about learning disabilities that I was not prepared to help design a plan for Samantha at this meeting.

"...the child we knew as bright and imaginative was coming home scared and unhappy."

At this first IEPC a large disparity in skills was discovered. We listened to the analysis and agreed with the professional recommendations. To protect her self-esteem we were advised not to pull her out of the classroom for special help. "She is so bright, she will be fine. Be happy it's not a problem with reading." What we ALL forgot to consider was her self-esteem if left in the classroom. Samantha was getting further and further behind her peer group. She was working harder and harder *to learn* less and less. We were still told not to worry, she could always use a calculator. It was assumed she knew enough about number relationships to know which buttons to push (bad assumption). Expecting her to hold her own with increasingly difficult material would begin to take its toll.

The happiest math experience Samantha had was in third grade - the year of multiplication tables. With her uncanny ability to memorize, she was a star. In spite of not understanding anything involved with the thought process, she learned that everyone cheered when she said 5x4=20. Because of this success, I naively thought her problems were solved.

Fourth, fifth and sixth grades brought different stories. She simply could not keep up with the building and application concepts. 5-3 were merely oddly shaped symbols. Coupled with this was a now pronounced inability to tell time, count money, or spell. I could sense that this very bright child was in very big trouble. She too knew that even though her grades were good, she was not really "getting it." She was failing to learn and it bothered her deeply. We had many trips to the doctor for stomach aches and many tears after school. As the grades and years progressed, so did the signs of stress. Panic and anxiety attacks began to surface. By the sixth grade, the disparity in skills could be likened to the Grand Canyon. She combined writing and thought patterns described as wise beyond her years with the inability to grasp simple numerical concepts.

During seventh grade, witnessing the increasing stress she was facing and the effect it was having on all parts of her life, we became determined to provide her with help.

"She was working harder and harder to learn less and less."

We knew we needed to get her labeled learning disabled to allow her access to a specially trained teacher in math. This was not without its frustrations. At one point, we were told the only way to get help was to have her fail. Samantha had been humiliated enough and that was not an acceptable answer. Fortunately, we had learned much over the years and were able to be far more capable advocates for our child.

At this second IEPC we learned there were tests and then there were tests. One showed her performing above grade level in math, another showed her performing at less than one percentile in certain areas. At our insistence yet another test was given that seemed to provide the most accurate assessment of her abilities. We had also made efforts to gain the support of the learning disabilities teacher, her general math teacher and her school guidance counselor. The combination of accurate test scores and advocates within the system was invaluable in attaining a more complete view of Samantha's problems. She qualified for help. This help was not gained without controversy, but I would urge all parents to become informed, to keep asking questions, to go after what you feel is right for your child. Do not lose sight of the fact that it is *you* who know your child best. We felt the prescription suggested by some, to progress her with occasional monitoring, was inappropriate. We knew this would lead to more failure and more anxiety. Most importantly, it offered no possible hope for her to learn.

Our daughter is now receiving the best of what schools and the IEPC process are all about. The value of having these specially trained teachers focus on the specific learning needs of a child and to implement appropriate remediation cannot be praised enough. Once we learned more about the nature of learning disabilities and became stronger advocates within the IEPC process, it became instrumental in defining a meaningful educational program for our daughter. It has placed her where she can learn. Samantha is a paradox, but by learning to work with the school and to raise concerns when necessary, we were able to create educational opportunities appropriate to her needs.

> *"I would urge all parents to keep trying, to go after what you feel is right for your child."*

I now have a better understanding of the root of our problem in getting help. Samantha's overall high academic performance made it difficult to believe she was truly learning disabled. The idea of average or above average academic functioning combined with a learning problem can be a difficult concept to accept. Fortunately, as more is learned about this combination, people like Dr. Susan Baum, Steve Owen and John Dixon are sharing their knowledge. The following quote from their book, To Be Gifted & Learning Disabled, helps define such children. "These students are struggling to stay at grade level. Their superior intellectual ability is working overtime to help compensate for weaknesses caused by an undiagnosed learning disability. In essence, their gift masks the disability and the disability masks the gift. These students are often difficult to find because they do not flag the need for attention by exceptional behavior."

Today, Samantha and this book are a wonderful example of what can happen when parents listen to their children, schools listen to parents, and all function as a team. Learning disabilities do not go away. Samantha will always be faced with challenges that most of us will never see. However, because of the knowledgeable people she has had the opportunity to work with, she has learned compensation skills and coping strategies that will make those challenges less formidable. This kind of help does not have to mean inventing new school programs, only looking at what is already available within a given system and generating teacher awareness about the ramifications of having a learning disability. In addition to being instrumental in getting the special help she needed, Samantha's counselor was also able to place her in an advanced creative writing class previously available only to older students. She finally had balance because both her strength and weakness were being tended. As her educational needs were appropriately addressed, all of her symptoms of stress disappeared. Now, she is a delightfully normal adolescent with a learning "difference" who has ups and downs and everything between. The symptoms of anxiety are gone.

"Those of us who learn through regular channels will probably never be able to comprehend the battles learning disabled children face..."

Those of us who learn through regular channels will probably never be able to comprehend the battles learning disabled children face on a day to day, minute to minute basis. Daily routines as simple as opening a locker and finding the right page number can be a mountain to climb for a child who has difficulty with memory and sequencing skills. Because of my daughter, I have been forced to try to understand these struggles and how hard these children must work to overcome them. As Dr. Mel Levine states in <u>Keeping a Head in School</u>, "Kids with learning problems think of themselves as one big mess of deficits, disorders, disabilities and weaknesses. They forget all about the things they do well."

To counter this, it is important for parents and teachers to become as informed as possible. To be persistent when the answers don't fit the questions. Because of the nature of learning disabilities, no two children have exactly the same problem. This makes diagnosing and planning difficult. We must remember that the child is not always the sum of the numbers that appear at the bottom of a standardized test. We need to remember to make room for the word "individual" in the IEPC process.

Help for parents is not limited to the IEPC. The LDA (Learning Disabilities Association) and the Orton Dyslexia Society are national organizations with state chapters. They are wonderful resources and I have learned much from them. There are also many good books on the topic of learning disabilities. Perhaps one of the greatest resources in your community are other parents. Networking with others who share a common concern can be a terrific source of support and information.

I would like to urge all parents and teachers to look deep inside their children and students. There is a seed hiding in all of them and this seed needs to be encouraged and nurtured. The most beautiful rose in our garden began from a tiny seed and the thorns around that rose were merely the obstacles we had to respectfully work around.

The following is a poem that Samantha wrote to a special teacher as a thank you. I would like to use it to thank all the people who have helped us along the way.

Elizabeth Abeel

Thank You

When the sun rose
from under its misty veil,
you were there to watch,
like the birds over the sea.
When the wind came quietly
and rested in your ear,
you listened, as the earth would at dawn.
When the rain fell,
you reached out with your hands
and let it wash everything away
like waves as they grasp the shore.
When the plain brown seed was planted,
you could already smell the fragrance of
the flower that was to come,
and you were proud
As a good gardener should be.

Thank you for believing
that there was a flower waiting inside
and for taking the time
to help
and watch it grow.
When the sun rose
from under its misty veil,
you were there to watch
and I am thankful.

Acknowledgments

This book could not have happened without the help and encouragement of many people. Our special thanks to our families: David and Zac Abeel; Carrie Craig Murphy and David, Jonathan, and Katherine Williams. Your patience and understanding were always appreciated. We are also indebted to G.F. "Skip" Bourdo, Lana Crandall, Mike Kelly, Dee Massaroni, Dave Millross, Jack Olson and Mary Pratt, without whom this would not be a success story. We deeply appreciate the time and suggestions of the many friends and colleagues who listened to us, encouraged us and helped critique and proofread our manuscript: Dr. Susan K. Baum, Charles and Susan Cady, Corinne Chabot, Laurie Davis, Dr. Donald Deshler, Jerry Dennis, Patricia Dolanski, Cathryn Drewry, Susan Galbraith, Helene Gruber, Jerry Jenkins, Dr. William Lakey, Dr. Mel Levine, Alex Moore, Jim Novak, Chris Okoren, Mary Beth Perkins, William Pringle, Mike Romstadt, William Shaw, Connie Sweeny, Dick and Peg Townsend, Barbara VenHorst, Martha Vreeland, Barb Webster, A.V. and Emmy Williams, John Robert Williams and Glenn Wolff. Sometimes it was only your enthusiasm that kept us going. A special thank you to Tom Woodruff for helping us to navigate new and unfamiliar waters.

Grateful acknowledgment is also made to the following for permission to quote from copyrighted material:

Baum, Dr. Susan K., Steve V. Owen and John Dixon, *To Be Gifted and Learning Disabled.* Mansfield
    Center, Connecticut: Creative Learning Press, Inc.,1991.

Levine, Dr. Mel, *Keeping A Head in School.* Cambridge: Educators Publishing Services, Inc., 1990.

Smith, Sally L., *Succeeding Against the Odds.* Los Angeles: Jeremy T. Tarcher, Inc., 1991.

Watercolors:	From the Collection of:	Writing:
Gabrielle's Flute Solo	Barbara and Michael Dennos	*What Once Was White*
Sunrise II	Private Collection	*Sunrise*
Song for Sunflowers	Private Collection	*Alone*
Neighborhood Fabric	John and Katherine Williams	*Quilt*
Theme Piece to Bagpipes	Delores Gilbert Pike	*Come All the Old*
Autumn Muse	Darryl and Gerrie Milarch	*Leaves in the Fall*
Silently I watched it spin upon the breeze...	Samantha Abeel	*Music of the Heart*
Violin Player	*Playing for the Birds* print series	*Music of the Heart*
There was but one sail ripped through the middle...	David and Roberta Williams	*Music of the Heart*
Voices in the Canyon Wind	Delores Gilbert Pike	*Voices of Ancestry*
Nightwind	Carolyn Lawrence Geer	*Shivers in the Blackness*
Trail of Ancestry	Kenneth and Jocelyn Lesperance	*If You Want to See*
Francisco Dons the Tree Robe	Barbara and Michael Dennos	*The Cloak*
Drawing the Curtain of Night	Delores Gilbert Pike	*Drawing the Curtain of Night*

Further Information

The following organizations can be very helpful for those with learning disabilities. Consult the National organization for the address of your state or local chapter.

Learning Disabilities Association
4156 Library Road
Pittsburgh, PA 15234

Learning Disabilities Association of Michigan
200 Museum Drive
Lansing, MI 48933-1905

Orton Dyslexia Society
Suite 382 Chester Building
8600 LaSalle Road
Baltimore, Maryland 21204-6020

For more information about the artist, contact:

Charles R. Murphy
True North Studio
518 W. 8th St.
Traverse City, MI 49684

For information about workshops and school or conference presentations contact:

Hidden Bay Productions
P.O. Box 86
Traverse City, MI 49685-0086
616-947-2058 or 616-271-3230

For our information:

We are sincerely interested in your comments about this book, whether it be suggestions, insights, or a story to share. If you have comments or would like to order additional copies of this book, you may write to us at:

Hidden Bay Publishing
P.O. Box 86
Traverse City, MI 49685-0086